ILLUMINATED
POEMS

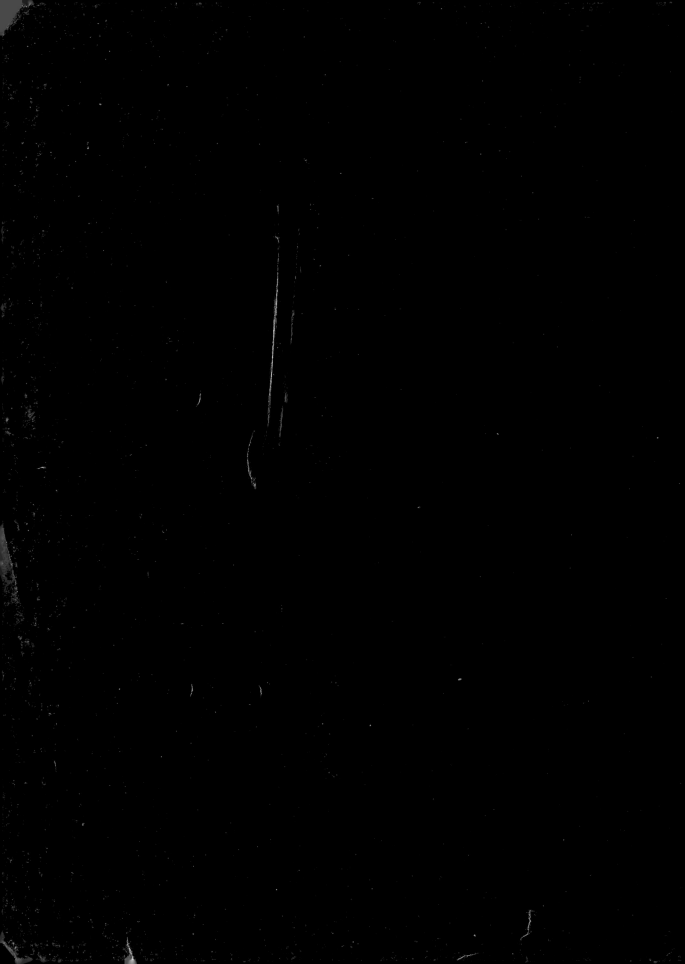

ILLUMINATED
POEMS

BY ALLEN GINSBERG

WITH PAINTINGS AND DRAWINGS BY
ERIC DROOKER

Thunder's Mouth Press

New York

Published by:

Thunder's Mouth Press
An Imprint of Avalon Publishing Group, Inc.
245 West 17th Street, 11th Floor
New York, NY 10010

Except from "America Again" and "Confession Is Dream for the Soul," which are published here for the first time, all poems can be found in the following Ginsberg anthologies: *Collected Poems, First Blues, White Shroud,* and *Cosmopolitan Greetings.* Thanks to the hospitable editors at *The New Yorker, The Nation,* and *New York Newsday* for first publishing recent poems. Spelling and punctuation are taken from original texts.

Some of Eric Drooker's illustrations were first published in *The New Yorker.*

First edition published by Four Walls Eight Windows in 1996.
Second edition published by Thunder's Mouth Press in 2006.

www.thundersmouth.com

Mumia Abu-Jamal, pictured on page 81, is a political prisoner and journalist on death row in Pennsylvania. For information visit www.Mumia.org.

Library of Congress Cataloging-in-Publication Data:
Ginsberg, Allen 1926–1997
Illuminated poems / by Allen Ginsberg
   p. cm.
   ISBN 1-56858-045-2 (cloth).—ISBN 1-56858-070-3 (trade paperback)
   I. Drooker, Eric, 1958–   . II. Title.
   PS3513.I74A6   1996
   811'.54—DC20   95-52059
                                                     CIP

Printed in China.

10 9 8 7 6 5 4 3 2 1

Cover and book design by Eric Drooker.
Text design by Acme Art, Inc.

*Dedicated to the prophets, visionaries
... and refugees of the 21st century.*

Contents

Introduction

Drooker's Illuminations

I first glimpsed Eric Drooker's odd name on posters pasted on fire-alarm sides, construction walls checkered with advertisements, & lamppost junction boxes in the vortex of Lower East Side Avenues leading to Tompkins Square Park, where radical social dislocation mixed homeless plastic tents with Wigstock transvestite dress-up anniversaries, Rastas sitting on benches sharing spliff, kids with purple Mohawks, rings in their noses ears eyebrows and bellybuttons, adorable or nasty skinheads, wives with dogs & husbands with children strolling past jobless outcasts, garbage, and a bandshell used weekly for folk-grunge concerts, anti-war rallies, squatters' rights protests, shelter for blanket-wrapped junkies & winos and political thunder music by Missing Foundation, commune-rockers whose logo, an overturned champagne glass with the slogan "The Party's Over," was spray-painted on sidewalks, apartments, brownstone and brick walled streets.

Eric Drooker's numerous block-print-like posters announced much local action, especially squatters' struggles and various mayoral-police attempts to destroy the bandshell & close the Park at night, driving the homeless into notoriously violence-corrupted city shelters. Tompkins Park had a long history of political protest going back before Civil War anti-draft mob violence, memorialized as ". . . a mixed surf of muffled sound, the atheist roar of riot," in Herman Melville's "The Housetop: A Night Piece (July 1863)."

I began collecting Drooker's posters soon after overcoming shock, seeing in contemporary images the same dangerous class conflict I'd remembered from childhood, pre-Hitler block print wordless novels by Frans Masereel and Lynd Ward. Ward's images of the solitary artist dwarfed by the canyons of a Wall Street Megalopolis lay shadowed behind my own vision of Moloch. What "shocked" me in Drooker's scratchboard prints was his graphic illustration of economic crisis similar to Weimar-American 1930's Depressions.

In our own era, as one Wall Street stockbroker noted, "Reagan put the nation in hock to the military," with resulting collapse of human values & social stability. Drooker illuminated the widely-noted impoverishment of underclass, "diminishing expectations" of middleclass city dwellers, and transfer of disproportionate shares of common wealth to those already rich. This economic information, including facts of multi-billion savings & loan bankruptcies paid for by federal funds, was reported in neutral tones by newspapers of record but Drooker illustrated the city's infrastructural stress, housing decay, homelessness, garbage-hunger and bitter suffering of marginalized families, Blacks and youth, with such vivid detail that the authoritarian reality horror of our contemporary dog-eat-dog Malthusian technoeconomic class-war became immediately visible.

". . . It is a question of genuine values, human worth, trustworthiness," Thomas Mann commented, introducing Frans Masereel's novel in woodcuts *Passionate Journey*. Drooker spent his childhood on East 14th Street & Avenue B, exploring the city early, observing "shopping bag ladies, stretch-cadillacs, screaming

unshaven men, junkies nodding, Third Avenue prostitutes look-
ing at themselves in rearview mirrors of parked cars." His maternal
grandparents were 1930's socialists, his mother taught in the
neighborhood's PS 19, on 11th Street & First Avenue, his father,
white-collar computer programmer, tripped him to art museums
all over the city.

1970's he attended Henry Street Settlement art classes,
graduated from Cooper Union, moved permanently to East 10th
Street close to Tompkins Park. Following family tradition he
organized rent strikes, supported local squats and tenant
organizing against police brutality. By 1980's working as freelance
artist for many leftist groups, with reputation as radical street
art-provocateur, he was arrested and thrown in District of
Columbia jail for postering. In "denial" of economic crisis, city
bureaucrats cracked down on Punk and political postering as a
"public nuisance." Xeroxed flyers were considered "illegal
graffiti."

By 1990's observant Op-ed editors at the N.Y. *Times* invited
him to contribute art for their pages, as did *The Nation, Village
Voice* and *Newsweek*. Under a new post-modern regime at *The
New Yorker*, he published many illustrations, even covers, includ-
ing a celebrated image of two bums standing huddled round a
bright garbage-can fire as big snowflakes fell under the Brooklyn
Bridge. His novel in pictures, *FLOOD!*, with its fantastic social
dreams, won an American Book Award.

Our collaboration volume began as byproduct of an illustra-
tion of my poem "The Lion For Real" for his St. Mark's Poetry
Project New Year's Day 1993 Benefit poster.

As I'd followed his work over a decade, I was flattered that so radical an artist of later generations found the body of my poetry still relevant, even inspiring. Our paths crossed often, we took part in various political rallies and poetical-musical entertainments, the idea of a sizable volume of illustrated poem-pictures rose. Eric Drooker himself did all the work choosing texts (thankfully including many odd lesser-known scribings) and labored several years to complete these *Illuminated Poems.*

Allen Ginsberg
Lower East Side
December 28, 1995

Prologue

The year was 1967 and I was an eight-year-old boy riding the crosstown bus with my mother.

The bus stopped on Avenue A, and a man with black-rimmed glasses and a big black beard entered alone and sat down in front of us.

My mother leaned over and whispered in my ear that the man in front of us was a famous poet.

I didn't know what to think. What did this mean? What did a famous poet do all day. . . write poems?

As the bus slowly moved forward I sat quietly, looking at the back of his balding head and wondering what he was thinking as we rolled west on 14th Street.

Eric Drooker
Lower East Side
January 15, 1996

ILLUMINATED
POEMS

The Eye Altering Alters All

Many seek and never see,
anyone can tell them why.
O they weep and O they cry
and never take until they try
unless they try it in their sleep
and never some until they die.
I ask many, they ask me.
This is a great mystery.

East Harlem, June-July 1948

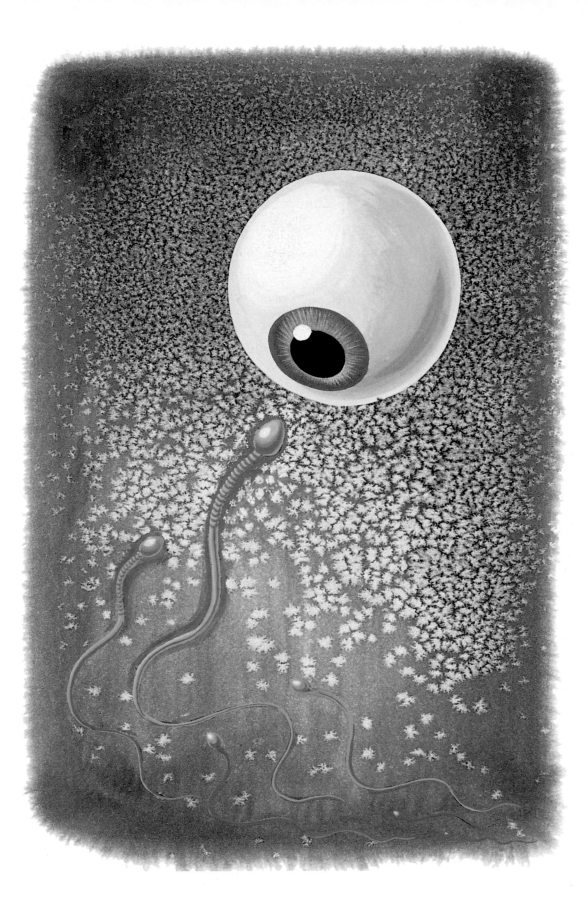

An Eastern Ballad

I speak of love that comes to mind:
The moon is faithful, although blind;
She moves in thought she cannot speak.
Perfect care has made her bleak.

I never dreamed the sea so deep,
The earth so dark; so long my sleep,
I have become another child.
I wake to see the world go wild.

1945-1949

A Mad Gleam

Go back to Egypt and the Greeks,
Where the wizard understood
The spectre haunted where man seeks
And spoke to ghosts that stood in blood.

Go back, go back to the old legend;
The soul remembers, and is true:
What has been most and least imagined,
No other, there is nothing new.

The giant Phantom is ascending
Toward its coronation, gowned
With music unheard, yet unending:
Follow the flower to the ground.

New York, January 1949

In Death, Cannot Reach What Is Most Near

We know all about death that we will ever know because we have all experienced the state before birth. Life seems a passage between two doors to the darkness. Both are the same and truly eternal, and perhaps it may be said that we meet in darkness. The nature of time is illuminated by this meeting of eternal ends.

It is amazing to think that thought and personality of man is perpetuated in time after his passage to eternity. And one time is all Time if you look at it out of the grave.

New York, Mid-1949

Song

The weight of the world
        is love.
Under the burden
        of solitude,
under the burden
        of dissatisfaction

        the weight
the weight we carry
        is love.

Who can deny?
        In dreams
it touches
        the body,
in thought
        constructs
a miracle,
        in imagination
anguishes
        till born
in human—

looks out of the heart
        burning with purity—
for the burden of life

is love,
but we carry the weight
        wearily,
and so must rest
in the arms of love
        at last,
must rest in the arms
        of love.

No rest
        without love,
no sleep
        without dreams
of love—
        be mad or chill
obsessed with angels
        or machines,
the final wish
        is love
—cannot be bitter,
        cannot deny,
cannot withhold
        if denied:

the weight is too heavy
        —must give
for no return

        as thought
is given
        in solitude
in all the excellence
        of its excess.

The warm bodies
        shine together
in the darkness,
        the hand moves
to the center
        of the flesh,
the skin trembles
        in happiness
and the soul comes
        joyful to the eye—

yes, yes,
        that's what
I wanted,
        I always wanted,
I always wanted,
        to return
to the body
        where I was born.

San Jose, 1954

Lay Down Yr Mountain

Lay down   Lay down yr mountain   Lay down God
Lay down   Lay down your music   Love lay down

Lay down   Lay down yr hatred   Lay yrself down
Lay down   Lay down your nation   Lay your foot on the rock

Lay down yr whole creation   Lay yr mind down
Lay down   Lay down yr empire   Lay your whole world down

Lay down your soul forever   Lay your vision down
Lay down yr bright body   Down your golden heavy crown

Lay down   Lay down yr magic hey!   Alchemist lay it down clear
Lay down your practice precisely   Lay down yr wisdom dear

Lay down yr skillful camera   Lay down yr image right
Lay down your brilliant image   Lay down light

Lay down   your ignorance   Roll yr wheel once more
Lay down yr empty suffering   Lay down yr Lion's Roar

October 31, 1975

Sunflower Sutra

I walked on the banks of the tincan banana dock and sat down
               under the huge shade of a Southern Pacific locomotive
               to look at the sunset over the box house hills and cry.
Jack Kerouac sat beside me on a busted rusty iron pole, compan-
               ion, we thought the same thoughts of the soul, bleak
               and blue and sad-eyed, surrounded by the gnarled steel
               roots of trees of machinery.
The oily water on the river mirrored the red sky, sun sank on top
               of final Frisco peaks, no fish in that stream, no hermit
               in those mounts, just ourselves rheumy-eyed and
               hung-over like old bums on the riverbank, tired and
               wily.
Look at the Sunflower, he said, there was a dead gray shadow
               against the sky, big as a man, sitting dry on top of a
               pile of ancient sawdust—
—I rushed up enchanted—it was my first sunflower, memories
               of Blake—my visions—Harlem
and Hells of the Eastern rivers, bridges clanking Joes Greasy
               Sandwiches, dead baby carriages, black treadless tires
               forgotten and unretreaded, the poem of the riverbank,
               condoms & pots, steel knives, nothing stainless, only
               the dank muck and the razor-sharp artifacts passing
               into the past—
and the gray Sunflower poised against the sunset, crackly bleak
               and dusty with the smut and smog and smoke of olden
               locomotives in its eye—

corolla of bleary spikes pushed down and broken like a battered
      crown, seeds fallen out of its face, soon-to-be-toothless
      mouth of sunny air, sunrays obliterated on its hairy
      head like a dried wire spiderweb,
leaves stuck out like arms out of the stem, gestures from the
      sawdust root, broke pieces of plaster fallen out of the
      black twigs, a dead fly in its ear,
Unholy battered old thing you were, my sunflower O my soul, I
      loved you then!
The grime was no man's grime but death and human locomotives,
all that dress of dust, that veil of darkened railroad skin, that smog
      of cheek, that eyelid of black mis'ry, that sooty hand
      or phallus or protuberance of artificial worse-than-
      dirt—industrial—modern—all that civilization spot-
      ting your crazy golden crown—
and those blear thoughts of death and dusty loveless eyes and ends
      and withered roots below, in the home-pile of sand and
      sawdust, rubber dollar bills, skin of machinery, the guts
      and innards of the weeping coughing car, the empty
      lonely tincans with their rusty tongues alack, what
      more could I name, the smoked ashes of some cock
      cigar, the cunts of wheelbarrows and the milky breasts
      of cars, wornout asses out of chairs & sphincters of
      dynamos—all these
entangled in your mummied roots—and you there standing
      before me in the sunset, all your glory in your form!
A perfect beauty of a sunflower! a perfect excellent lovely sun-
      flower existence! a sweet natural eye to the new hip

moon, woke up alive and excited grasping in the sunset shadow sunrise golden monthly breeze!

How many flies buzzed round you innocent of your grime, while you cursed the heavens of the railroad and your flower soul?

Poor dead flower? when did you forget you were a flower? when did you look at your skin and decide you were an impotent dirty old locomotive? the ghost of a locomotive? the specter and shade of a once powerful mad American locomotive?

You were never no locomotive, Sunflower, you were a sunflower!

And you Locomotive, you are a locomotive, forget me not!

So I grabbed up the skeleton thick sunflower and stuck it at my side like a scepter,

and deliver my sermon to my soul, and Jack's soul too, and anyone who'll listen,

—We're not our skin of grime, we're not our dread bleak dusty imageless locomotive, we're all golden sunflowers inside, blessed by our own seed & hairy naked accomplishment-bodies growing into mad black formal sunflowers in the sunset, spied on by our eyes under the shadow of the mad locomotive riverbank sunset Frisco hilly tincan evening sitdown vision.

Berkeley, 1955

Manhattan Thirties Flash

Long stone streets inanimate, repetitive machine Crash cookie-
　　　　cutting
dynamo rows of soulless replica Similitudes brooding tank-like in
　　　　Army Depots
Exactly the same exactly the same exactly the same with no
　　　　purpose but grimness
& overwhelming force of robot obsession, our slaves are not alive
& we become their sameness as they surround us—the long stone
　　　　streets inanimate,
crowds of executive secretaries alighting from subway 8:30 A.M.
bloodflow in cells thru elevator arteries & stairway glands to
　　　　typewriter consciousness,
Con Ed skyscraper clock-head gleaming gold-lit at sun dusk.

1968

Morning

Ugh! the planet screams
Doves in rusty cornice-
            castles peer
down on auto crossroads,
        a junkey in white jacket
wavers in yellow light on
        way to a negro in bed
Black smoke flowing on roofs, terrific
                city coughing—
garbage can lids music over
        truck whine on E. 5th St.
Ugh! I'm awake again—
        dreary day ahead
what to do?—Dull letters
        to be answered
an epistle to M. Duchamp
more me all day the same
clearly

            Q. "Do you want to live or die?"
            A. "I don't know"
        said Julius after 12 years
            · State Hospital

Ugh! cry negroes in Harlem

Ugh! cry License Inspectors, Building
       Inspectors, Police Congressmen,
       Undersecretaries of Defense.
Ugh! Cries Texas Mississippi!
Ugh! Cries India
Ugh! Cries US
       Well, who knows?

O flowing copious!
      total Freedom! To
Do what? to blap! to
      embarrass! to conjoin
Locomotive blossoms to Leafy
      purple vaginas.
To be dull! ashamed! shot!
      Finished! Flopped!
To say Ugh absolutely mean-
      ingless here
To be a big bore! even to
      myself! Fulla shit!

Paper words! Fblup! Fizzle! Droop!
Shut your big fat mouth!
Go take a flying crap in the
      rain!
Wipe your own ass! Bullshit!
You big creep! Fairy! Dopy
      Daffodil! Stinky Jew!

Mr. Professor! Dirty Rat! Fart!

Honey! Darling! Sweetie pie!
Baby! Lovey! Dovey! Dearest!
My own! Buttercup! O Beautiful!
Doll! Snookums! Go fuck
            yourself,
         everybody Ginsberg!
And when you've exhausted
         that, go forward?
Where? kiss my ass!

O Love, my mouth against
     a black policeman's breast.

New York, 1963

Howl

For Carl Solomon

I.

I saw the best minds of my generation destroyed by madness,
        starving hysterical naked,

dragging themselves through the negro streets at dawn looking
        for an angry fix,

angelheaded hipsters burning for the ancient heavenly connection
        to the starry dynamo in the machinery of night,

who poverty and tatters and hollow-eyed and high sat up smoking
        in the supernatural darkness of cold-water flats floating
        across the tops of cities contemplating jazz,

who bared their brains to Heaven under the El and saw
        Mohammedan angels staggering on tenement roofs
        illuminated,

who passed through universities with radiant cool eyes hallucinat-
        ing Arkansas and Blake-light tragedy among the schol-
        ars of war,

who were expelled from the academies for crazy & publishing
        obscene odes on the windows of the skull,

who cowered in unshaven rooms in underwear, burning their
        money in wastebaskets and listening to the Terror
        through the wall,

who got busted in their pubic beards returning through Laredo
        with a belt of marijuana for New York,

who ate fire in paint hotels or drank turpentine in Paradise Alley,
        death, or purgatoried their torsos night after night

with dreams, with drugs, with waking nightmares, alcohol and
       cock and endless balls,
incomparable blind streets of shuddering cloud and lightning in
       the mind leaping toward poles of Canada & Paterson,
       illuminating all the motionless world of Time between,
Peyote solidities of halls, backyard green tree cemetery dawns,
       wine drunkenness over the rooftops, storefront bor-
       oughs of teahead joyride neon blinking traffic light,
       sun and moon and tree vibrations in the roaring winter
       dusks of Brooklyn, ashcan rantings and kind king light
       of mind,
who chained themselves to subways for the endless ride from
       Battery to holy Bronx on benzedrine until the noise of
       wheels and children brought them down shuddering
       mouth-wracked and battered bleak of brain all drained
       of brilliance in the drear light of Zoo,
who sank all night in submarine light of Bickford's floated out
       and sat through the stale beer afternoon in desolate
       Fugazzi's, listening to the crack of doom on the hydro-
       gen jukebox,
who talked continuously seventy hours from park to pad to bar
       to Bellevue to museum to the Brooklyn Bridge,
a lost battalion of platonic conversationalists jumping down the
       stoops off fire escapes off windowsills off Empire State
       out of the moon,
yacketayakking screaming vomiting whispering facts and memo-
       ries and anecdotes and eyeball kicks and shocks of
       hospitals and jails and wars,

whole intellects disgorged in total recall for seven days and nights
     with brilliant eyes, meat for the Synagogue cast on the
     pavement,
who vanished into nowhere Zen New Jersey leaving a trail of
     ambiguous picture postcards of Atlantic City Hall,
suffering Eastern sweats and Tangerian bone-grindings and mi-
     graines of China under junk-withdrawal in Newark's
     bleak furnished room,
who wandered around and around at midnight in the railroad
     yard wondering where to go, and went, leaving no
     broken hearts,
who lit cigarettes in boxcars boxcars boxcars racketing through
     snow toward lonesome farms in grandfather night,
who studied Plotinus Poe St. John of the Cross telepathy and bop
     kabbalah because the cosmos instinctively vibrated at
     their feet in Kansas,
who loned in through the streets of Idaho seeking visionary indian
     angels who were visionary indian angels,
who thought they were only mad when Baltimore gleamed in
     supernatural ecstasy,
who jumped in limousines with the Chinaman of Oklahoma on
     the impulse of winter midnight streetlight smalltown
     rain,
who lounged hungry and lonesome through Houston seeking jazz
     of sex or soup, and followed the brilliant Spaniard to
     converse about America and Eternity, a hopeless task,
     and so took ship to Africa,
who disappeared into the volcanoes of Mexico leaving behind

nothing but the shadow of dungarees and the lava and
        ash of poetry scattered in fireplace Chicago,
who reappeared on the West Coast investigating the FBI in beards
        and shorts with big pacifist eyes sexy in their dark skin
        passing out incomprehensible leaflets,
who burned cigarette holes in their arms protesting the narcotic
        tobacco haze of Capitalism,
who distributed Supercommunist pamphlets in Union Square
        weeping and undressing while the sirens of Los Alamos
        wailed them down, and wailed down Wall, and the
        Staten Island ferry also wailed,
who broke down crying in white gymnasiums naked and
        trembling before the machinery of other skeletons,
who bit detectives in the neck and shrieked with delight in
        policecars for committing no crime but their own wild
        cooking pederasty and intoxication,
who howled on their knees in the subway and were dragged off
        the roof waving genitals and manuscripts,
who let themselves be fucked in the ass by saintly motorcyclists,
        and screamed with joy,
who blew and were blown by those human seraphim, the sailors,
        caresses of Atlantic and Caribbean love,
who balled in the morning in the evenings in rosegardens and the
        grass of public parks and cemeteries scattering their
        semen freely to whomever come who may,
who hiccuped endlessly trying to giggle but wound up with a sob
        behind a partition in a Turkish Bath when the blond
        & naked angel came to pierce them with a sword,

who lost their loveboys to the three old shrews of fate the one eyed
shrew of the heterosexual dollar the one eyed shrew
that winks out of the womb and the one eyed shrew
that does nothing but sit on her ass and snip the
intellectual golden threads of the craftsman's loom,

who copulated ecstatic and insatiate with a bottle of beer a
sweetheart a package of cigarettes a candle and fell off
the bed, and continued along the floor and down the
hall and ended fainting on the wall with a vision of
ultimate cunt and come eluding the last gyzym of
consciousness,

who sweetened the snatches of a million girls trembling in the
sunset, and were red eyed in the morning but prepared
to sweeten the snatch of the sunrise, flashing buttocks
under barns and naked in the lake,

who went out whoring through Colorado in myriad stolen night-
cars, N.C., secret hero of these poems, cocksman and
Adonis of Denver—joy to the memory of his innumer-
able lays of girls in empty lots & diner backyards,
moviehouses' rickety rows, on mountaintops in caves
or with gaunt waitresses in familiar roadside lonely
petticoat upliftings & especially secret gas-station so-
lipsisms of johns, & hometown alleys too,

who faded out in vast sordid movies, were shifted in dreams, woke
on a sudden Manhattan, and picked themselves up out
of basements hungover with heartless Tokay and hor-
rors of Third Avenue iron dreams & stumbled to
unemployment offices,

who walked all night with their shoes full of blood on the
      snowbank docks waiting for a door in the East River
      to open to a room full of steamheat and opium,
who created great suicidal dramas on the apartment cliff-banks of
      the Hudson under the wartime blue floodlight of the
      moon & their heads shall be crowned with laurel in
      oblivion,
who ate the lamb stew of the imagination or digested the crab at
      the muddy bottom of the rivers of Bowery,

who wept at the romance of the streets with their pushcarts full
of onions and bad music,
who sat in boxes breathing in the darkness under the bridge, and
rose up to build harpsichords in their lofts,
who coughed on the sixth floor of Harlem crowned with flame
under the tubercular sky surrounded by orange crates
of theology,
who scribbled all night rocking and rolling over lofty incantations
which in the yellow morning were stanzas of gibberish,
who cooked rotten animals lung heart feet tail borscht & tortillas
dreaming of the pure vegetable kingdom,
who plunged themselves under meat trucks looking for an egg,
who threw their watches off the roof to cast their ballot for
Eternity outside of Time, & alarm clocks fell on their
heads every day for the next decade,
who cut their wrists three times successively unsuccessfully, gave
up and were forced to open antique stores where
they thought they were growing old and cried,
who were burned alive in their innocent flannel suits on Madison

Avenue amid blasts of leaden verse & the tanked-up
clatter of the iron regiments of fashion & the nitroglyc-
erine shrieks of the fairies of advertising & the mustard
gas of sinister intelligent editors, or were run down by
the drunken taxicabs of Absolute Reality,

who jumped off the Brooklyn Bridge this actually happened and
walked away unknown and forgotten into the ghostly
daze of Chinatown soup alleyways & firetrucks, not
even one free beer,

who sang out of their windows in despair, fell out of the subway
window, jumped in the filthy Passaic, leaped on ne-
groes, cried all over the street, danced on broken
wineglasses barefoot smashed phonograph records of
nostalgic European 1930s German jazz finished the
whiskey and threw up groaning into the bloody toilet,
moans in their ears and the blast of colossal
steamwhistles,

who barreled down the highways of the past journeying to each
other's hotrod-Golgotha jail-solitude watch or Bir-
mingham jazz incarnation,

who drove crosscountry seventytwo hours to find out if I had a
vision or you had a vision or he had a vision to find out
Eternity,

who journeyed to Denver, who died in Denver, who came back
to Denver & waited in vain, who watched over Denver
& brooded & loned in Denver and finally went away
to find out the Time, & now Denver is lonesome for
her heroes,

who fell on their knees in hopeless cathedrals praying for each
        other's salvation and light and breasts, until the soul
        illuminated its hair for a second,

who crashed through their minds in jail waiting for impossible
        criminals with golden heads and the charm of reality
        in their hearts who sang sweet blues to Alcatraz,

who retired to Mexico to cultivate a habit, or Rocky Mount to
        tender Buddha or Tangiers to boys or Southern Pacific
        to the black locomotive or Harvard to Narcissus to
        Woodlawn to the daisychain or grave,

who demanded sanity trials accusing the radio of hypnotism &
        were left with their insanity & their hands & a hung
        jury,

who threw potato salad at CCNY lecturers on Dadaism and
        subsequently presented themselves on the granite steps
        of the madhouse with shaven heads and harlequin
        speech of suicide, demanding instantaneous lobotomy,

and who were given instead the concrete void of insulin Metrazol
        electricity hydrotherapy psychotherapy occupational
        therapy pingpong & amnesia,

who in humorless protest overturned only one symbolic pingpong
        table, resting briefly in catatonia,

returning years later truly bald except for a wig of blood, and tears
        and fingers, to the visible madman doom of the wards
        of the madtowns of the East,

Pilgrim State's Rockland's and Greystone's foetid halls, bickering
        with the echoes of the soul, rocking and rolling in the
        midnight solitude-bench dolmen-realms of love,

dream of life a nightmare, bodies turned to stone as
        heavy as the moon,
with mother finally ******, and the last fantastic book flung out
        of the tenement window, and the last door closed at 4
        A.M. and the last telephone slammed at the wall in
        reply and the last furnished room emptied down to the
        last piece of mental furniture, a yellow paper rose
        twisted on a wire hanger in the closet, and even that
        imaginary, nothing but a hopeful little bit of halluci-
        nation—
ah, Carl, while you are not safe I am not safe, and now you're
        really in the total animal soup of time—
and who therefore ran through the icy streets obsessed with a
        sudden flash of the alchemy of the use of the ellipsis
        catalog a variable measure & the vibrating plane,
who dreamt and made incarnate gaps in Time & Space through
        images juxtaposed, and trapped the archangel of the
        soul between 2 visual images and joined the elemental
        verbs and set the noun and dash of consciousness
        together jumping with sensation of Pater Omnipotens
        Aeterne Deus
to recreate the syntax and measure of poor human prose and stand
        before you speechless and intelligent and shaking with
        shame, rejected yet confessing out the soul to conform
        to the rhythm of thought in his naked and endless
        head,
the madman bum and angel beat in Time, unknown, yet putting

down here what might be left to say in time come after
    death,
and rose reincarnate in the ghostly clothes of jazz in the goldhorn
    shadow of the band and blew the suffering of America's
    naked mind for love into an eli eli lamma lamma
    sabacthani saxophone cry that shivered the cities down
    to the last radio
with the absolute heart of the poem of life butchered out of their
    own bodies good to eat a thousand years.

II.

What sphinx of cement and aluminum bashed open their skulls
    and ate up their brains and imagination?
Moloch! Solitude! Filth! Ugliness! Ashcans and unobtainable
    dollars! Children screaming under the stairways! Boys
    sobbing in armies! Old men weeping in the parks!
Moloch! Moloch! Nightmare of Moloch! Moloch the loveless!
    Mental Moloch! Moloch the heavy judger of men!
Moloch the incomprehensible prison! Moloch the crossbone
    soulless jailhouse and Congress of sorrows! Moloch
    whose buildings are judgment! Moloch the vast stone
    of war! Moloch the stunned governments!
Moloch whose mind is pure machinery! Moloch whose blood is
    running money! Moloch whose fingers are ten armies!
    Moloch whose breast is a cannibal dynamo! Moloch
    whose ear is a smoking tomb!
Moloch whose eyes are a thousand blind windows! Moloch whose
    skyscrapers stand in the long streets like endless

Jehovahs! Moloch whose factories dream and croak in the fog! Moloch whose smokestacks and antennae crown the cities!

Moloch whose love is endless oil and stone! Moloch whose soul is electricity and banks! Moloch whose poverty is the specter of genius! Moloch whose fate is a cloud of sexless hydrogen! Moloch whose name is the Mind!

Moloch in whom I sit lonely! Moloch in whom I dream Angels! Crazy in Moloch! Cocksucker in Moloch! Lacklove and manless in Moloch!

Moloch who entered my soul early! Moloch in whom I am a consciousness without a body! Moloch who frightened me out of my natural ecstasy! Moloch whom I abandon! Wake up in Moloch! Light streaming out of the sky!

Moloch! Moloch! Robot apartments! invisible suburbs! skeleton treasuries! blind capitals! demonic industries! spectral nations! invincible madhouses! granite cocks! monstrous bombs!

They broke their backs lifting Moloch to Heaven! Pavements, trees, radios, tons! lifting the city to Heaven which exists and is everywhere about us!

Visions! omens! hallucinations! miracles! ecstasies! gone down the American river!

Dreams! adorations! illuminations! religions! the whole boatload of sensitive bullshit!

Breakthroughs! over the river! flips and crucifixions! gone down the flood! Highs! Epiphanies! Despairs! Ten years'

animal screams and suicides! Minds! New loves! Mad
generation! down on the rocks of Time!
Real holy laughter in the river! They saw it all! the wild eyes! the
holy yells! They bade farewell! They jumped off the
roof! to solitude! waving! carrying flowers! Down to the
river! into the street!

III.

Carl Solomon! I'm with you in Rockland
where you're madder than I am
I'm with you in Rockland
where you must feel very strange
I'm with you in Rockland
where you imitate the shade of my mother
I'm with you in Rockland
where you've murdered your twelve secretaries
I'm with you in Rockland
where you laugh at this invisible humor
I'm with you in Rockland
where we are great writers on the same dreadful
typewriter
I'm with you in Rockland
where your condition has become serious and is
reported on the radio
I'm with you in Rockland
where the faculties of the skull no longer admit the
worms of the senses

I'm with you in Rockland
> where you drink the tea of the breasts of the spinsters
> of Utica

I'm with you in Rockland
> where you pun on the bodies of your nurses the harpies
> of the Bronx

I'm with you in Rockland
> where you scream in a straightjacket that you're losing
> the game of the actual pingpong of the abyss

I'm with you in Rockland
> where you bang on the catatonic piano the soul is
> innocent and immortal it should never die ungodly in
> an armed madhouse

I'm with you in Rockland
> where fifty more shocks will never return your soul to
> its body again from its pilgrimage to a cross in the void

I'm with you in Rockland
> where you accuse your doctors of insanity and plot the
> Hebrew socialist revolution against the fascist national
> Golgotha

I'm with you in Rockland
> where you will split the heavens of Long Island and
> resurrect your living human Jesus from the superhu-
> man tomb

I'm with you in Rockland
> where there are twentyfive thousand mad comrades all
> together singing the final stanzas of the Internationale

I'm with you in Rockland
>   where we hug and kiss the United States under our
>   bedsheets the United States that coughs all night and
>   won't let us sleep
I'm with you in Rockland
>   where we wake up electrified out of the coma by our
>   own souls' airplanes roaring over the roof they've come
>   to drop angelic bombs the hospital illuminates itself
>   imaginary walls collapse   O   skinny legions run out-
>   side   O starry-spangled shock of mercy the eternal war
>   is here   O   victory forget your underwear we're free
I'm with you in Rockland
>   in my dreams you walk dripping from a sea-journey on
>   the highway across America in tears to the door of my
>   cottage in the Western night

>   *San Francisco, 1955-1956*

Footnote to Howl

Holy! Holy! Holy! Holy! Holy! Holy! Holy! Holy! Holy! Holy!
Holy! Holy! Holy! Holy! Holy!
The world is holy! The soul is holy! The skin is holy! The nose is
holy! The tongue and cock and hand and asshole holy!
Everything is holy! everybody's holy! everywhere is holy! everyday
is in eternity! Everyman's an angel!
The bum's as holy as the seraphim! the madman is holy as you
my soul are holy!
The typewriter is holy the poem is holy the voice is holy the hearers
are holy the ecstasy is holy!
Holy Peter holy Allen holy Solomon holy Lucien holy Kerouac
holy Huncke holy Burroughs holy Cassady holy the
unknown buggered and suffering beggars holy the
hideous human angels!
Holy my mother in the insane asylum! Holy the cocks of the
grandfathers of Kansas!
Holy the groaning saxophone! Holy the bop apocalypse! Holy the
jazzbands marijuana hipsters peace peyote pipes &
drums!
Holy the solitudes of skyscrapers and pavements! Holy the cafe-
terias filled with the millions! Holy the mysterious
rivers of tears under the streets!
Holy the lone juggernaut! Holy the vast lamb of the middleclass!
Holy the crazy shepherds of rebellions! Who digs Los
Angeles IS Los Angeles!
Holy New York Holy San Francisco Holy Peoria & Seattle Holy

Paris Holy Tangiers Holy Moscow Holy Istanbul!

Holy time in eternity holy eternity in time holy the clocks in space
holy the fourth dimension holy the fifth International
holy the Angel in Moloch!

Holy the sea holy the desert holy the railroad holy the locomotive
holy the visions holy the hallucinations holy the mira-
cles holy the eyeball holy the abyss!

Holy forgiveness! mercy! charity! faith! Holy! Ours! bodies! suf-
fering! magnanimity!

Holy the supernatural extra brilliant intelligent kindness of the
soul!

Berkeley, 1955

New York Blues

On Neal's Ashes

Delicate eyes that blinked blue Rockies all ash
nipples, Ribs I touched w/ my thumb are ash
mouth my tongue touched once or twice all ash
bony cheeks soft on my belly are cinder, ash
earlobes & eyelids, youthful cock tip, curly pubis
breast warmth, man palm, high school thigh,
baseball bicept arm, asshole anneal'd to silken skin
                        all ashes, all ashes again.

August 1968

Punk Rock Your My Big Crybaby

I'll tell my deaf mother on you! Fall on the floor
and eat your grandmother's diapers! Drums,
Whatta lotta Noise you want a Revolution?
Wanna Apocalypse? Blow up in Dynamite Sound?
I can't get excited, Louder! Viciouser!
Fuck me in the ass! Suck me! Come in my ears!
I want those pink Abdominal bellybuttons!
Promise you'll murder me in the gutter with Orgasms!
I'll buy a ticket to your nightclub, I wanna get busted!
50 years old I wanna Go! with whips & chains & leather!
Spank me! Kiss me in the eye! Suck me all over
from Mabuhay Gardens to CBGB's coast to coast
Skull to toe Gimme yr electric guitar naked,
Punk President, eat up the FBI w/ yr big mouth.

Mabuhay Gardens, May 1977

Get It?

Get beat up on TV squirming on the ground for driving irregular
Get bombed in Philadelphia by helicopters with your little babies
Get kicked in the street by Newark police and charged w/riot
Get assassinated by a jerk while FBI sleeps with itself
Get shot by a stringer for the CIA & blame it on Fair Play for
    Cuba Committee
Get bumped off by an errandboy for Cuban drug kingpins, friend
    of the Feds & Dallas cops
Get caught paying off Contras with coke money while Acting U.S.
    Drug War Czar
Get busted for overcharging Iranians on secret warplane sales
Get convicted of lying to Congress about off-the-shelf dirty wars ·
    in Central America
Get 12 billion dollars for a drug bureaucracy and double the
    number of addicts
Get a million people in prison in the land of the free
Get the electric chair & gas chamber for unpopular crimes
Organize *Citizens for Decency Through Law* rob your own phony
    bank several billion dollars get sent to jail

May 1992
New York

Capitol Air

I don't like the government where I live
I don't like dictatorship of the Rich
I don't like bureaucrats telling me what to eat
I don't like Police dogs sniffing round my feet

I don't like Communist Censorship of my books
I don't like Marxists complaining about my looks
I don't like Castro insulting members of my sex
Leftists insisting we got the mystic Fix

I don't like Capitalists selling me gasoline Coke
Multinationals burning Amazon trees to smoke
Big Corporation takeover media mind
I don't like the Top-bananas that're robbing Guatemala banks
        blind

I don't like K.G.B. Gulag concentration camps
I don't like the Maoists' Cambodian Death Dance
20 Million were killed by Stalin Secretary of Terror
He has killed our old Red Revolution for ever

I don't like Anarchists screaming Love Is Free
I don't like the C.I.A. they killed John Kennedy
Paranoiac tanks sit in Prague and Hungary
But I don't like counterrevolution paid for by the C.I.A.

Tyranny in Turkey or Korea Nineteen Eighty
I don't like Right Wing Death Squad Democracy
Police State Iran Nicaragua yesterday
Laissez-faire please Government keep your secret police offa me

I don't like Nationalist Supremacy White or Black
I don't like Narcs & Mafia marketing Smack
The General bullying Congress in his tweed vest
The President building up his Armies in the East & West

I don't like the Crown's Official Secrets Act
You can get away with murder in the Government that's a fact
Security cops teargassing radical kids
In Switzerland or Czechoslovakia God Forbids

In America was Attica in Russia was Lubianka Wall
In China if you disappear you wouldn't know yourself at all
Arise Arise you citizens of the world use your lungs
Talk back to the Tyrants all they're afraid of is your tongues

Two hundred Billion dollars inflates World War
In United States every year They're asking for more
Russia's had as much in tanks and laser planes
Give or take Fifty Billion we could blow out everybody's brains

School's broke down 'cause History changes every night
Half the Free World nations are Dictatorships of the Right
Socialism worked in Scandanavia, Bud
The Communist world was stuck together with prisoners' blood

The Generals say they know something worth fighting for
They never say what till they start an unjust war
Iranian hostage Media Hysteria sucked
The Shah ran away with 9 Billion Iranian bucks

Kermit Roosevelt and his U.S. dollars overthrew Mossadegh
They wanted his oil then they got Ayatollah's dreck
They put in the Shah and they trained his police the Savak
All Iran was our hostage quarter-century That's right Jack

Bishop Romero wrote President Carter to stop
Sending guns to El Salvador's Junta so he got shot
Ambassador White blew the whistle on the White House lies
Reagan called him home cause he looked in the dead nuns' eyes

Half the voters didn't vote they knew it was too late
Newspaper headlines called it a big Mandate
Some people voted for Reagan eyes open wide
3 out of 4 didn't vote for him That was a Landslide

Truth may be hard to find but Falsehood's easy
Read between the lines our Imperialism is sleazy
But if you think the People's State is your Heart's Desire
Jump right back in the frying pan from the fire

The System the System in Russia now China the same
Criticize the System in Budapest lose your name
Coca Cola Pepsi Cola in Russia & China come true
Khrushchev yelled in Hollywood "We will bury You"

America and Russia wanted to bomb themselves Okay
Everybody dead on both sides   Everybody pray
All except the Generals in caves where they can hide
And fuck each other in the ass waiting for the next free ride

No hope Communism no hope Capitalism Yeah
Everybody's lying on both sides Nyeah nyeah nyeah
The bloody iron curtain of American Military Power
Was a mirror image of Russia's red Babel-Tower

Jesus Christ was spotless but was Crucified by the Mob
Law & Order Herod's hired soldiers did the job
Flowerpower's fine but innocence has got no Protection
The man who shot John Lennon had a Hero-worshipper's
                    connection

The moral of this song is that the world is in a horrible place
Scientific Industry devours the human race
Police in every country armed with Tear Gas & TV
Secret Masters everywhere bureaucratize for you & me

Terrorists and police together build a lowerclass Rage
Propaganda murder manipulates the upperclass Stage
Can't tell the difference 'tween a turkey & a provocateur
If you're feeling confused the Government's in there for sure

Aware Aware wherever you are   No Fear
Trust your heart Don't ride your Paranoia dear
Breathe together with an ordinary mind
Armed with Humor Feed & Help Enlighten   Woe Mankind

Frankfurt-New York, December 15, 1980

Pentagon Exorcism

"No taxation without representation"

Who represents my body in Pentagon? Who spends
my spirit's billions for war manufacture? Who
levies the majority to exult unwilling in Bomb
Roar? *"Brainwash!"* Mind-fear! Governor's language!
"Military-Industrial-Complex!" President's language!
Corporate voices jabber on electric networks building
body-pain, chemical ataxia, physical slavery
to diaphanoid Chinese Cosmic-eye Military Tyranny
movie hysteria—Pay my taxes? No *Westmoreland* wants
to be Devil, others die for his General Power
sustaining hurt millions in house security
tuning to images on TV's separate universe where
peasant manhoods burn in black & white forest
villages—represented less than myself by Magic
Intelligence influence matter-scientists' *Rockefeller*
bank telephone war investment Usury Agency
executives jetting from *McDonnell Douglas* to *General Dynamics*
over smog-shrouded metal-noised treeless cities
patrolled by radio fear with tear gas, businessman!
Go spend your bright billions for this suffering!
Pentagon wake from planet-sleep! Apokatastasis!
Spirit Spirit Dance Dance Spirit Spirit Dance!
Transform Pentagon skeleton to maiden-temple O Phantom

Guevara! Om Gate Gate Paragate Parasamgate Bodhi Svaha!
Anger Control your Self feared Chaos, suffocation
body-death in Capitols caved with stone radar sentinels!
Back! Back! Back! Central Mind-machine Pentagon reverse
consciousness! Hallucination manifest! A million Americas
gaze out of man-spirit's naked Pentacle! Magnanimous
reaction to signal Peking, isolate Space-beings!

Milan, September 29, 1967

Love Forgiven

War Profit Litany

To Ezra Pound

These are the names of the companies that have made money
        from this war
nineteenhundredsixtyeight Annodomini   fourthousandeighty
        Hebraic
These Corporations have profited by merchandising skinburning
        phosphorus or shells fragmented to thousands of
        fleshpiercing needles
and here listed money millions gained by each combine for
        manufacture
and here are gains numbered, index'd swelling a decade, set in
        order,
here named the Fathers in office in these industries, telephones
        directing finance,
names of directors, makers of fates, and the names of the stock-
        holders of these destined Aggregates,
and here are the names of their ambassadors to the Capital,
        representatives to legislature, those who sit drinking in
        hotel lobbies to persuade,
and separate listed, those who drop Amphetamines with military,
        gossip, argue, and persuade
suggesting policy naming language proposing strategy, this done
        for fee as ambassadors to Pentagon, consultants to
        military, paid by their industry:
and these are the names of the generals & captains military, who

now thus work for war goods manufacturers;

and above these, listed, the names of the banks, combines, investment trusts that control these industries:

and these are the names of the newspapers owned by these banks

and these are the names of the airstations owned by these combines;

and these are the numbers of thousands of citizens employed by these businesses named;

and the beginning of this accounting is 1958 and the end 1968, that statistic be contained in orderly mind, coherent & definite,

and the first form of this litany begun first day December 1967 furthers this poem of these States.

December 1, 1967

When the Light Appears

Lento

You'll bare your bones you'll grow you'll pray you'll only know
When the light appears, boy, when the light appears
You'll sing & you'll love you'll praise blue heavens above
When the light appears, boy, when the light appears
You'll whimper & you'll cry you'll get yourself sick and sigh
You'll sleep & you'll dream you'll only know what you mean
When the light appears, boy, when the light appears
You'll come & you'll go, you'll wander to and fro
You'll go home in despair you'll wonder why'd you care
You'll stammer & you'll lie you'll ask everybody why
You'll cough and you'll pout you'll kick your toe with gout
You'll jump you'll shout you'll knock your friends about
You'll bawl and you'll deny & announce your eyes are dry
You'll roll and you'll rock you'll show your big hard cock
You'll love & you'll grieve & one day you'll come believe
As you whistle & you smile the lord made you worthwhile
You'll preach and you'll glide on the pulpit in your pride
Sneak & slide across the stage like a river in high tide
You'll come fast or come on slow just the same you'll never know
When the light appears, boy, when the light appears

May 3, 1987, 2:30 A.M.

Tears

I'm crying all the time now.
I cried all over the street when I left the Seattle Wobbly Hall.
I cried listening to Bach.
I cried looking at the happy flowers in my backyard, I cried at the
        sadness of the middle-aged trees.

Happiness exists I feel it.
I cried for my soul, I cried for the world's soul.
The world has a beautiful soul.
God appearing to be seen and cried over. Overflowing heart of
        Paterson.

Seattle, February 2, 1956

The Lion for Real

"Soyez muette pour moi, Idole contemplative..."

I came home and found a lion in my living room
Rushed out on the fire escape screaming Lion! Lion!
Two stenographers pulled their brunette hair and banged the
          window shut
I hurried home to Paterson and stayed two days.

Called up my old Reichian analyst
who'd kicked me out of therapy for smoking marijuana
"It's happened" I panted "There's a Lion in my room"
"I'm afraid any discussion would have no value" he hung up.

I went to my old boyfriend we got drunk with his girlfriend
I kissed him and announced I had a lion with a mad gleam in my
          eye
We wound up fighting on the floor I bit his eyebrow & he kicked
          me out
I ended masturbating in his jeep parked in the street moaning
          "Lion."

Found Joey my novelist friend and roared at him "Lion!"
He looked at me interested and read me his spontaneous ignu
          high poetries
I listened for lions all I heard was Elephant Tiglon Hippogriff
          Unicorn Ants

But figured he really understood me when we made it in Ignaz
        Wisdom's bathroom.

But next day he sent me a leaf from his Smoky Mountain retreat
"I love you little Bo-Bo with your delicate golden lions
But there being no Self and No Bars therefore the Zoo of your
        dear Father hath no Lion
You said your mother was mad don't expect me to produce the
        Monster for your Bridegroom."

Confused dazed and exalted bethought me of real lion starved in
       his stink in Harlem
Opened the door the room was filled with the bomb blast of his
       anger
He roaring hungrily at the plaster walls but nobody could hear
       him outside thru the window
My eye caught the edge of the red neighbor apartment building
       standing in deafening stillness

We gazed at each other his implacable yellow eye in the red halo
       of fur
Waxed rheumy on my own but he stopped roaring and bared a
       fang greeting.
I turned my back and cooked broccoli for supper on an iron gas
       stove
boilt water and took a hot bath in the old tub under the sink
       board.

He didn't eat me, tho I regretted him starving in my presence.
Next week he wasted away a sick rug full of bones wheaten hair
       falling out
enraged and reddening eye as he lay aching huge hairy head on
       his paws
by the egg-crate bookcase filled up with thin volumes of Plato, &
       Buddha.

Sat by his side every night averting my eyes from his hungry
       motheaten face

stopped eating myself he got weaker and roared at night while I
    had nightmares
Eaten by lion in bookstore on Cosmic Campus, a lion myself
    starved by Professor Kandisky, dying in a lion's flop-
    house circus,
I woke up mornings the lion still added dying on the floor—
    "Terrible Presence!" I cried "Eat me or die!"

I got up that afternoon—walked to the door with its paw on the
    wall to steady its trembling body
Let out a soul-rending creak from the bottomless roof of his
    mouth
thundering from my floor to heaven heavier than a volcano at
    night in Mexico
Pushed the door open and said in a gravelly voice "Not this time
    Baby—but I will be back again."

Lion that eats my mind now for a decade knowing only your
    hunger
Not the bliss of your satisfaction O roar of the Universe how am
    I chosen
In this life I have heard your promise I am ready to die I have
    served
Your starved and ancient Presence O Lord I wait in my room at
    your Mercy.

Paris, March 1958

I'm a Prisoner of Allen Ginsberg

Who is this Slave Master makes
            me answer letters in his name
Write poetry year after year, keep up
                appearances
This egotist whose file cabinets
            leave no room for more
            pictures of Me?
How escape his clutches, his public sound,
            bank accounts, Master Charge
            interest
Who's this politician hypnotized my life
            with his favors
Petty friends & covert Nemesis, dead heroes and
            living ghosts hanging around
waiting Genius handout?
Why's this guy oblige me to sit
                meditating,
shine rocknroll Moon on Midwest Collegetown
            stages blind in overhead
            spotlights
bawling out of tune into giant microphones
makes me go down suck teenage boys
I declare a new life, how can I pay all
            his debts
next month's rent on his body,
            bald & panicky, with Pyronie's disease
Cartilage stuff grown an inch inside
            his cock root,
non-malignant.

Karme-Choling, April 4, 1983, 12:15 A.M.

Fighting Phantoms Fighting Phantoms

Fighting phantoms we have car wrecks on Hollywood Freeway

Fighting phantoms th'Egyptians mummified Pharaohs & rich
businessmen

Fighting phantoms a young Scotsman wore tennis shoes on the
battleship deck

Fighting phantoms William S. Burroughs wrote umpteen novels

Fighting giant phantoms David picked up his sling

Fighting phantoms Chögyam Trungpa Vidyadara founded
Shambhala Kingdom in North America

Fighting phantoms pay federal taxes few write tax refusal forms

Fighting phantoms a Son of God ascended his wooden cross

Fighting summer phantoms muscular young musicians jumped
up screaming in the twilit movie theatre

Fighting phantoms Siddhartha meditated under a Bo tree

Fighting phantoms mysticism entered into the Catholic Church
of Hollywood

Fighting phantoms a hundred thousand kids ordered purple
Mohawks

Fighting phantoms various fairies chased adolescent athletes
through steam bath locker rooms

Fighting phantoms the ruling class blew up the military budget,
244 Billion dollars 1985—of the tax pie 63% if past
military debt interest & pensions're added in

Fighting phantoms Ronald Reagan sent cocaine armadas to
Central America

Fighting phantoms poets who smoked cigarettes denounced
cigarettes—

Fighting phantoms New York Times printed thousands of
editorial pages

Fighting phantoms Adolf Hitler shot more Methamphetamine &
chewed the Bunker rug

Fighting phantoms thousand of poets become rather good at acid
satire

Fighting phantoms Jimmy Dean stepped on the gas, Orson
Welles ordered another cheesecake

Fighting phantoms Ernest Hemingway shotgunned his brain

Fighting phantoms Ezra Pound hated some Jews some hated
Pound

Fighting phantoms Truman dropped two Atom Bombs

Fighting phantoms Einstein invented the theory of relativity

Mid-August 1983

This Form of Life Needs Sex

I will have to accept women
           if I want to continue the race,
     kiss breasts, accept
     strange hairy lips behind
                buttocks,
Look in questioning womanly eyes
           answer soft cheeks,
bury my loins in the hang of pearplum
           fat tissue
               I had abhorred
before I give godspasm Babe leap
           forward thru death—
Between me and oblivion an unknown
                woman stands;
Not the Muse but living meat-phantom,
a mystery scary as my fanged god
           sinking its foot in its gullet &
vomiting its own image out of its ass
—This woman Futurity I am pledge to
           born not to die,

but issue my own cockbrain replica Me-Hood
                again—For fear of the Blot?
Face of Death, my Female, as I'm sainted
                to my very bone,
I'm fated to find me a maiden for
                        ignorant Fuckery—
flapping my belly & smeared with Saliva
                shamed face flesh & wet,
—have long droopy conversations
                in Cosmical Duty boudoirs,
                        maybe bored?
Or excited New Prospect, discuss
                her, Futurity, my Wife
                My Mother, Death, My only
                        hope, my very Resurrection
Woman
                herself, why have I feared
                to be joined true
                embraced beneath the Panties of Forever
in with the one hole that repelled me 1937 on?
—Pulled down my pants on the porch showing
                my behind to cars passing in rain—
& She be interested, this contact with Silly new Male
                that's sucked my loveman's cock
in Adoration & sheer beggary romance-awe
                gulp-choke Hope of Life come
and buggered myself innumerably boy-yangs
                gloamed inward so my solar plexus

feel godhead in me like an open door—

Now that's changed my decades body old
tho' admiring male thighs at my brow,
    hard love pulsing thru my ears,
    stern buttocks upraised
       for my masterful Rape
    that were meant for a private shit
       if the Army were All—

But no more answer to life
            than the muscular statue
      I felt up its marbles
      envying Beauty's immortality in the
            museum of Yore—
You can fuck a statue but you can't
      have children
You can joy man to man but the Sperm
            comes back in a trickle at dawn
      in a toilet on the 45th Floor—
& Can't make continuous mystery out of that
            finished performance
                        & ghastly thrill
      that ends as began,
                  stupid reptile squeak
      denied life by Fairy Creator
            become Imaginary
      because he decided not to incarnate
            opposite—Old Spook
who didn't want to be a baby & die,
            didn't want to shit and scream
            exposed to bombardment on a
                  Chinese RR track
and grow up to pass his spasm on
      the other half of the Universe—
Like a homosexual capitalist afraid of the masses—
and that's my situation, Folks—

                              New York, April 12, 1961

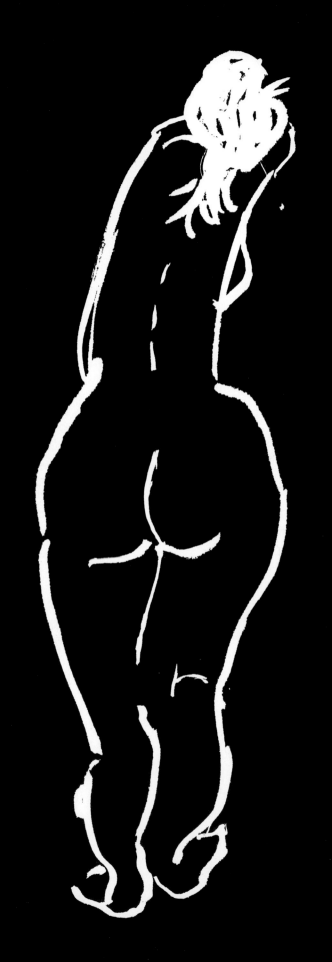

Birdbrain!

Birdbrain runs the World!

Birdbrain is the ultimate product of Capitalism

Birdbrain chief bureaucrat of Russia, yawning,

Birdbrain ran FBI 30 years appointed by F. D. Roosevelt and
never chased Cosa Nostra!

Birdbrain apportions wheat to be burned, keep prices up on the
world market!

Birdbrain lends money to Developing Nation police-states thru
the International Monetary Fund!

Birdbrain never gets laid on his own he depends on his office to
pimp for him

Birdbrain offers brain transplants in Switzerland

Birdbrain wakes up in middle of night and arranges his sheets

I am Birdbrain!

I rule Russia Yugoslavia England Poland Argentina United States
El Salvador

Birdbrain multiples in China!

Birdbrain inhabits Stalin's corpse inside the Kremlin wall

Birdbrain dictates petrochemical agriculture in Afric desert re-
gions!

Birdbrain lowers North California's water table sucking it up for
Orange County Agribusiness Banks

Birdbrain harpoons whales and chews blubber in the tropics

Birdbrain clubs baby harp seals and wears their coats to Paris

Birdbrain runs the Pentagon his brother runs the CIA, Fatass
Bucks!

Birdbrain writes and edits *Time Newsweek Wall Street Journal Pravda Izvestia*

Birdbrain is Pope, Premier, President, Commissar, Chairman, Senator!

Birdbrain voted Reagan President of the United States!

Birdbrain prepares Wonder Bread with refined white flour!

Birdbrain sold slaves, sugar, tobacco, alcohol

Birdbrain conquered the New World and murdered mushroom god Xochopili on Popocatepetl!

Birdbrain was President when a thousand mysterious students were machinegunned at Tlatelulco

Birdbrain sent 20,000,000 intellectuals and Jews to Siberia, 15,000,000 never got back to the Stray Dog Café

Birdbrain wore a mustache & ran Germany on Amphetamines the last year of World War II

Birdbrain conceived the Final Solution to the Jewish Problem in Europe

Birdbrain carried it out in Gas Chambers

Birdbrain borrowed Lucky Luciano the Mafia from jail to secure Sicily for U.S. Birdbrain against the Reds

Birdbrain manufactured guns in the Holy Land and sold them to white goyim in South Africa

Birdbrain supplied helicopters to Central America generals, kill a lot of restless Indians, encourage a favorable business climate

Birdbrain began a war of terror against Israeli Jews

Birdbrain sent out Zionist planes to shoot Palestinian huts outside Beirut

Birdbrain outlawed Opiates on the world market

Birdbrain formed the Black Market in Opium

Birdbrain's father shot skag in hallways of the Lower East Side

Birdbrain organized Operation Condor to spray poison fumes on
the marijuana fields of Sonora

Birdbrain got sick in Harvard Square from smoking Mexican grass

Birdbrain arrived in Europe to Conquer cockroaches with
Propaganda

Birdbrain became a great International Poet and went around the
world praising the Glories of Birdbrain

I declare Birdbrain to be victor in the Poetry Contest

He built the World Trade Center on New York Harbor waters
without regard where the toilets emptied—

Birdbrain began chopping down the Amazon Rainforest to build
a woodpulp factory on the river bank

Birdbrain in Iraq attacked Birdbrain in Iran

Birdbrain in Belfast throws bombs at his mother's ass

Birdbrain wrote *Das Kapital* ! authored the *Bible* ! penned *The
Wealth of Nations* !

Birdbrain's humanity, he built the Rainbow Room on top of
Rockefeller Center so we could dance

He invented the Theory of Relativity so Rockwell Corporation
could make Neutron Bombs at Rocky Flats in Colo-
rado

Birdbrain's going to see how long he can go without coming

Birdbrain thinks his dong will grow big that way

Birdbrain sees a new Spy in the Market Platz in Dubrovnik
outside the Eyeglass Hotel—

Birdbrain wants to suck your cock in Europe, he takes life very
    seriously, brokenhearted you won't cooperate—
Birdbrain goes to heavy duty Communist Countries so he can get
    KGB girlfriends while the sky thunders—
Birdbrain realized he was Buddha by meditating
Birdbrain's afraid he's going to blow up the planet so he wrote
    this poem to be immortal—

Hotel Subrovka, Dubrovnik, October 14, 1980, 4:30 A.M.

America Again

6% Worlds Population consumes 40% world's raw materials
acrid smog over New York seen from Grand Central Parkway
           across bridges to Chrysler's Spire
brimstone over Los Angeles, Hollywood hills in brown gas
black soot over Chicago, Plastic bustees against the iron fences in
           Tompkins Park.

These 51 states to be "A Model" for the world?
If 6% consumes 40% of world's timber, beef, uranium, chrome,
           oil
What should the 94% rest aim for? Equal prosperity?
Our Wall street rises as the Amazon's burnt down?
Do we enjoy prosperity at the expense of other cultures?
Do we maintain this comfort at expense of Central America,
           Mexico, Peru, West Africa?

7/11/89 Tues eve

New Stanzas for *Amazing Grace*

I dreamed I dwelled in a homeless place
Where I was lost alone
Folk looked right through me into space
And passed with eyes of stone

O homeless hand on many a street
Accept this change from me
A friendly smile or word is sweet
As fearless charity

Woe workingman who hears the cry
And cannot spare a dime
Nor look into a homeless eye
Afraid to give the time

So rich or poor no gold to talk
A smile on your face
The homeless ones where you may walk
Receive amazing grace

I dreamed I dwelled in a homeless place
Where I was lost alone
Folk looked right through me into space
And passed with eyes of stone

4/2/94

Jumping the Gun on the Sun

Sincerity
is the key
to living
in Eternity

If you love
Heav'n above
Hold your ground,
Look around
Hear the sound
of television
No derision,
Smell your blood
taste your good
bagels & lox
Wash your sox
& touch wood,
It's understood
This is it
wild wit
Make your love
on earth above,
home of the brave,
Save yr grave
for future days
Present here
nothing to fear
No need to sigh
no need to die

before your time
mentally whine
stupidly dine
on your own meat
That's what's neat
Mortally great
Immortally sweet
Incredibly deep
makes you weep
Just this once
Don't be a dunce
Take your cap
off Hear my rap

Sincerity
is the key
to living
in Eternity

Makes you wise
in your own eyes
makes the body
not seem shoddy
Makes your soul
completely whole
empty, final
indefinable
Mobile, total-
ly undeniable

Affirmative action
for no faction
for all men
women too,
mother brother,
even for you
Dead soul'd, sick
but really quick
with breath & thick
with blood in yr prick
Walking alive
on Riverside Drive
up on Broadway
shining gay
in New York
waving your dork
waving your mind
or living behind
your meaty masque
magnificent task
all you could ask
as if pure space
gave you a place
in Eternity—
To see the City
Stand all day
Shine all night
Bright starlight
streaming the height
Watery lawn

misty at dawn
warmed by the sun
Bathed in the moon
green grasses of June
80 times only
Don't be lonely
Roses are live
Cockroaches thrive
in plastic garbage
maggots salvage
your dead meat
Horses eat
golden Hay
in golden day
Young kids jump
in the City dump
Take the lump
in your throat
and sing out
yr holy note
of heart's delight
in living light
Day & Night

Sincerity
is the key
to Bliss in this
Eternity

April 5, 1985

Rock Song

I'm up in the lightning tower
Blake is re-fighting Milton below
African Americans yelling at Latinos
With bombs crack wanna blow

African Americans with babies at their breasts
Europeans drinking coffee cashing checks
Vietnamese & Chinese behaving correct
Koreans and Texans thumping their chests

I'm up in the lightning tower
Could stay up here a hundred years
Shouting orders thru a diamond megaphone
Till the blood rain turns to humor tears

I'm up in the lightning tower
The spiritual war goes on
There's a million Caesars climbing up the stairs
I gotta fight them with one hard on

I'm up in the lightning window
I can see the blare of the bombs
The noisier the surplus airplanes thunder
The more I sit down calm

Up on the lightning rooftop
It's raining human bones and blood
I haven't got a holy umbrella
Is there anything I can do that's any good?

I'm dancing on the lightning cloud
I don't know how I got the power
I kept hearing everybody screaming
& lay down to sleep dream for one hour

Lightning tower lightning ocean
Lightning window, lightning cloud
Lightning solitude lightning delusion
Lightning consciousness in the crowd

Journals 5/25/90

Gospel Nobel Truths

Born in this world   Sit   you sit down
You got to suffer   Breathe when you breathe
Everything changes   Lie Down   you lie down
You got no soul   Walk where you walk

Try to be gay   Talk when you talk
Ignorant   Happy   Cry when you cry
You get the blues   Lie down   you lie down
You eat jellyroll   Die when you die

There is one Way   Look when you look
You take the high road   Hear what you hear
In your big Wheel   Taste what you taste   here
8 steps you fly   Smell what you smell

Look at the View   Touch what you touch
Right to horizon   Think what you think
Talk to the sky   Let go let it go   slow
Act like you talk   Earth Heaven & Hell

Work like the sun   Die when you die
Shine in your heaven   Die when you die
See what you done   Lie down   you lie down
Come down & walk   Die when you die

New York Subway, October 17, 1975

The Ballad of the Skeletons

Said the Presidential skeleton
I won't sign the bill
Said the Speaker skeleton
Yes you will

Said the Representative skeleton
I object
Said the Supreme Court skeleton
Whaddya expect

Said the Military skeleton
Buy Star Bombs
Said the Upperclass skeleton
Starve unmarried moms

Said the Yahoo skeleton
Stop dirty art
Said the Ring Wing skeleton
Forget about yr heart

Said the Gnostic skeleton
The Human Form's divine
Said the Christian Coalition skeleton
No it's not it's mine

Said the Buddha skeleton
Compassion is wealth
Said the Corporate skeleton
It's bad for your health

Said the Old Christ skeleton
Care for the Poor
Said the Son of God skeleton
AIDS needs cure

Said the Homophobe skeleton
Gay folk suck
Said the Heritage Policy skeleton
Blacks're outta luck

Said the Macho skeleton
Women in their place
Said the Fundamentalist skeleton
Increase human race

Said the Right-to-Life skeleton
Foetus has a soul
Said Pro-Choice skeleton
Shove it up your hole

Said the Downsized skeleton
Robots got my job
Said the Tough-on-Crime skeleton
Tear-gas the mob

Said the Governor skeleton
Cut school lunch
Said the Mayor skeleton
Eat the budget crunch

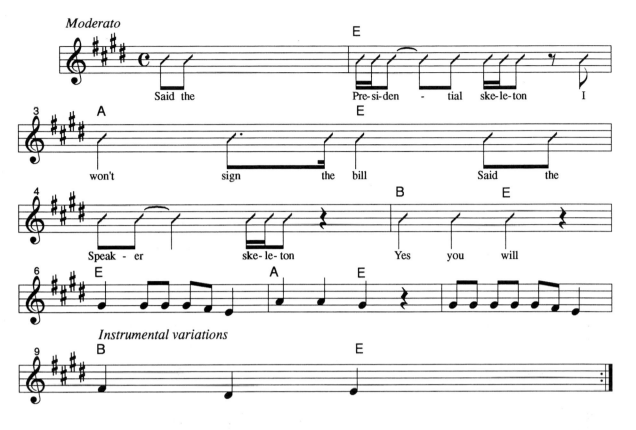

Moderato

Said the Pre-si-den - tial ske-le-ton I won't sign the bill Said the Speak-er ske-le-ton Yes you will

Instrumental variations

Said the Neo-Conservative skeleton
Homeless off the street!
Said the Free Market skeleton
Use 'em up for meat

Said the Think Tank skeleton
Free Market's the way
Said the Savings & Loan skeleton
Make the State pay

Said the Chrysler skeleton
Pay for you & me
Said the Nuke Power skeleton
& me & me & me

Said the Ecologic skeleton
Keep Skies blue
Said the Multinational skeleton
What's it worth to you?

Said the NAFTA skeleton
Get rich, Free Trade,
Said the Maquiladora skeleton
Sweat shops, low paid

Said the rich GATT skeleton
One world, high tech
Said the Underclass skeleton
Get it in the neck

Said the World Bank skeleton
Cut down your trees
Said the I.M.F. skeleton
Buy American cheese

Said the Underdeveloped skeleton
Send me rice
Said Developed Nations' skeleton
Sell your bones for dice

Said the Ayatollah skeleton
Die writer die
Said Joe Stalin's skeleton
That's no lie

Said the Petrochemical skeleton
Roar Bombers roar!
Said the Psychedelic skeleton
Smoke a dinosaur

Said Nancy's skeleton
Just say No
Said the Rasta skeleton
Blow Nancy Blow

Said Demagogue skeleton
Don't smoke pot
Said Alcoholic skeleton
Let your liver rot

Said the Junkie skeleton
Can't we get a fix?
Said the Big Brother skeleton
Jail the dirty tricks

Said the Mirror skeleton
Hey good looking
Said the Electric Chair skeleton
Hey what's cooking?

Said the Talkshow skeleton
Fuck you in the face
Said the Family Values skeleton
My family values mace

Said the N.Y. *Times* skeleton
That's not fit to print
Said the C.I.A. skeleton
Cantcha take a hint?

Said the Network skeleton
Believe my lies
Said the Advertising skeleton
Don't get wise!

Said the Media skeleton
Believe you me
Said the Couch-Potato skeleton
What me worry?

Said the TV skeleton
Eat sound bites
Said the Newscast skeleton
That's all Goodnight

2/12-16/95

Father Death Blues

Confession Is Dream For the Soul

Woke to pee, I was in bed, bandaged,
I was sore, I'd confessed, been
amputated, mutilated, wrapped in gauze,
recovering in prison hospital, soul
emptied — nothing more to fear, secrets
revealed — for Meat I'd murdered
for Money stole parts of bodies,
razor'd open cattle and fish, eaten
and discarded bloody pulp entrails
Now I was revenged, now impotent,
prisoner, nothing more to hide, no
longer doomed. What was my sin?
What didn't I know? Was the ordeal over?

from Journals
2/15/92 2:53 AM

Allen Ginsberg

4/5/91

About the Author

ALLEN GINSBERG's signal poem "Howl" overcame censorship to become one of the most widely read poems of the century. Born in Newark, New Jersey, in 1926, he was crowned Prague May King in 1965, then expelled by Czech police and simultaneously placed on the FBI's Dangerous Security List. Ginsberg traveled to and taught in the people's Republic of China, the Soviet Union, Scandinavia, and Eastern Europe, where he received Yugoslavia's Struga Poetry Festival "Golden Wreath" in 1986. He was a member of the American Institute of Arts and Letters and was co-founder of the Jack Kerouac School of Disembodied Poetics at the Naropa Institute, the first accredited Buddhist college in the Western world. He was winner of the Harriet Monroe Poetry Award given by the University of Chicago in 1991 and in 1993 received France's "Chevalier de l'Ordre des Arts et Lettres." He lived for over thirty years on Manhattan's Lower East Side, where he died at home in 1997.

About the Artist

ERIC DROOKER's paintings are frequently seen on covers of *The New Yorker* and in various art collections throughout the U.S. and Europe. He is a third generation New Yorker, who lived for decades on Manhattan's Lower East Side, where he befriended Allen Ginsberg on the street. His powerful graphics are used by activists throughout the world to protest corporate militarism and economic injustice. Drooker is the author of two graphic novels, *FLOOD! A Novel in Pictures* (winner of the American Book Award), and *Blood Song: A Silent Ballad.*

www.Drooker.com